EXPLORING AFRICAN CIVILIZATIONS™

DISCOVERING
THE EMPIRE
OF MALI

PHILIP WOLNY

Published in 2014 by The Rosen Publishing Group, Inc.
29 East 21st Street, New York, NY 10010

Library of Congress Cataloging-in-Publication Data

Wolny, Philip.
Discovering the Empire of Mali/Philip Wolny.—First edition.
      pages cm.—(Exploring African civilizations)
ISBN 978-1-4777-1883-4 (library binding)
1. Mali (Empire)—History—Juvenile literature. 2. Mali (Empire)—Civilization—Juvenile literature. 3. Mali (Empire)—Kings and rulers—Juvenile literature. I. Title.
DT532.2.W65 2014
966.2017—dc23

                                                              2013020102

Manufactured in the United States of America

CPSIA Compliance Information: Batch #W14YA: For further information, contact Rosen Publishing, New York, New York, at 1-800-237-9932.

A portion of the material in this book has been derived from *The Empire of Mali* by Carol Thompson.

CONTENTS

INTRODUCTION

One of the largest empires the world has ever known, the Empire of Mali flourished in West Africa from 1235 CE until 1464 CE. It is also referred to as the Manden Kurufaba (after the predominant ethnic group of the region, the Mandinka or Malinke). The empire remains well known for its wealth and its significant cultural influence, still felt hundreds of years later, both in modern Mali and its neighbors. The language, laws, and customs of the Empire of Mali spread throughout West Africa and along the Niger River, creating an enduring legacy that continues to influence and characterize the region centuries after the empire's end.

The Empire of Mali was located in the Sahel, a dry grassland region that lies between the Sahara Desert to the north and the forest regions to the south. In the forests, close to the source of the Niger River, lay the gold mines of Bambuk and Bure. Beyond the Sahara in northern Africa lay the wealthy coastal cities along the Mediterranean Sea.

Located between these two sources of wealth, the Sahel was ideally situated as a trading center for goods from both regions. As a result, several cities developed in this area. They became rich and powerful by taxing all the products traded in their territory.

The traders from the north and east who crossed the Sahara Desert via camel were mostly Berbers, desert peoples belonging to several different Islamic sects. The most valuable product they transported was salt, which they moved by camel and exchanged for gold. Salt was worth its weight in gold because

Pictured here is the inner courtyard of the Grand Mosque of Jenne in northern Mali, a nation with a rich and varied history that has preserved many of its historical treasures.

it is essential for a healthful diet and for food preservation, particularly in the hot Saharan climate. Many other goods crossed the Sahel, including slaves, ivory, animal skins from the south, and luxury products from the Mediterranean and the East.

Initially, the Empire of Ghana, which collapsed 150 years before the Empire of Mali rose to power, controlled the vast trade networks and major urban centers of the Sahel. Over time, however, reduction in its gold supplies, along with extended periods of drought, weakened that state's influence. The empire's trade links were also compromised by fighting among the various Berber groups. Finally, the Almoravid Berbers from Morocco defeated the Empire of Ghana in 1076. The weakened empire fell into chaos when its minor kings, all of whom had been part of the empire, struggled for control. The strongest leader emerging from this conflict was Sumanguru, king of the Susu people.

Sumanguru was in turn conquered by Sundiata, who ruled the then-small Kingdom of Mali. A leader and skillful negotiator, Sundiata reunited the region's peoples. Following the recipe for success that had made the Empire of Ghana great, Sundiata restored trade and founded the Empire of Mali.

The Empire of Mali enjoyed peace and prosperity. Its cities, including Niani, Jenne, Walata, Timbuktu, and Gao, became famous as centers of trade, culture, and learning. It was one of the richest and largest empires the world has ever seen, and its fame spread throughout Europe, Arabia, and Asia. It flourished until the second half of the fifteenth century, when it fell into decline. The dynastic line of royal succession was broken, and a series of obscure rulers reigned over an increasingly embattled territory. As the former Empire of Mali disintegrated into three separate realms, the Songhay Empire rose to fill the power void. Finally, by the end of the sixteenth century, the once fantastically wealthy, powerful, and influential Malian Empire was reduced to a small city-state.

CHAPTER ONE

Pre-Imperial Mali

The story of how Mali grew from a loose confederation of peoples into an influential and wealthy empire begins in West Africa during the thirteenth century. At the height of its power, the empire included most of the modern nations of Mali and Senegal, along with sections of Mauritania and Guinea. It arose out of the remains of a smaller, neighboring regional power, the Empire of Ghana, which had existed for about four centuries. The Empire of Mali eventually incorporated the neighboring territories of other tribes and rulers. Its peoples shared much in common with their neighbors, which aided this territorial expansion.

The Empire of Mali—like the Empire of Ghana—was built by Mandé-speaking peoples who spoke similar languages and shared a common culture. Ghana was built by the Soninke; the Empire of Mali was built by the Mandinka people (also known as Malinke or Mandingo). Other peoples who contributed to the rise of the Empire of Mali included Berber traders (such as the Tuareg), Fulbe (or Fulani) herdsmen, Arab merchants and scholars, and Bozo, Somono, and Sorko fishermen.

The Mandinka word *mali* means "hippopotamus," but it eventually came to mean "the place where the king lives." One Malian legend describes how Sundiata, who expanded the smaller Kingdom of Mali into a large empire, transformed himself into a hippopotamus in the Sankarani River.

Early Historical Accounts

Two griots perform with traditional instruments in the town of Sofara.

Information on the history of the Empire of Mali comes from early accounts by Arab writers, archaeologists, and the stories of griots, traditional oral historians of West Africa. Griots memorize long historical accounts called epics and pass them down through the generations by word of mouth. They employ music, poetry, drama, and dance to both entertain and educate. Griots play a stringed instrument called a kora.

With their koras and songs, griots challenge and inspire their listeners to match or surpass the heroic deeds of their ancestors. Griots also held important political and administrative roles in the Empire of Mali. They defended the empire's constitution and its legal principles, and they served as advisers to kings and as tutors to princes.

Mali's Early Rulers

Mandinka history describes how, before the founding of the Mali Empire, the Mandinka were divided into twelve clans,

Pictured here is a plate of a classic Islamic text, *The Life of the Prophet*, located at the New York Public Library. Malians take pride in their collections of such precious Islamic artifacts.

10 | Discovering the Empire of Mali

each made up of hunters, blacksmiths, or artisans. Each clan was ruled by its own king, and they were often at war with one another. To end the hostilities, the twelve kings formed a royal council and elected a *mansa*, or high king, uniting the twelve kingdoms as one.

The first rulers of the Mali Kingdom belonged to the Keita clan, and its first king was Latal Kalabi. The Keita clan claimed it could trace its historical origins back to Bilal Ibn Rabah, an Ethiopian who was a companion to the prophet Muhammad, the most important figure in Islam. Some accounts claim that Latal Kalabi's grandson, Lahilatul Kalabi, was the first black ruler to make the hajj. This is a pilgrimage to the holy city of Mecca that all Muslims who are able are required to take at least once during their lifetime.

Sundiata, founder of the Empire of Mali, followed later. He established the new capital of the Mali Kingdom—soon to become the Mali Empire—at his birthplace, the city of Niani, which was located somewhere along the Sankarani River.

Kangaba: A Spiritual Center

The original center of the Mali Kingdom was at Kangaba. The sacred shrine, the Mandeblo, remains there today. After Sundiata defeated the Susu, all of the Mandinka chiefs gathered at this shrine and swore allegiance to him.

Every seven years, Mandé peoples from throughout West Africa still gather at the Mandeblo for special ceremonies. The Mandeblo is also known as the Kaaba, sharing its name with the sacred shrine of Islam located in Mecca. This is because for several centuries a large proportion of the Mandé peoples have

This Kaba-blon, or shrine, located in Kangaba, the former capital of Mali's kingdom, belonged to Mali's famous Keita clan.

been Muslims. The guardians of the Mandeblo sanctuary belong to the Kadesi branch of the Keita clan, which traces its line of descent from Sundiata.

During the ceremonies at Kangaba, symbols are painted on the walls of the shrine, accompanied by performers reenacting the Mandé myth of creation. Griots tell sacred stories that describe the invention of speech, farming, and the crafts of blacksmithing and weaving. The latter two are regarded as the foundations of Mandé civilization.

The Mandé consider all creative people to be blessed. Their myths describe how the Creator, Maa Ngala, created the world

THE SPREAD OF ISLAM IN MALI

The Islamic faith had existed for centuries before spreading to the peoples of West Africa. The Empire of Mali was built from many religions and cultures, and even early on, Muslims held prominent posts in the royal court as advisers and counselors. Later, its leaders would embrace Islam more completely.

Scholars believe that Malians and other West Africans converted to Islam for several reasons. Economic motivations may have played a role because of the wealth and prestige of Muslim North African traders who helped Mali become prosperous. Others were drawn by Islam's spiritual message, which, like Christianity, stressed equality among people. Still others point out that literacy among practicing Muslims provided them with a competitive advantage at court as they helped to build the administrative framework of the Empire of Mali.

by speaking just a few words. He intentionally left his statement unfinished, giving creative people the task of completing it in the future. In Mandé society, artists of all kinds play a vital role and are seen as forever forming and reforming the world.

In addition, the high level of craftsmanship of the Mandé peoples helped set the stage for their success in forming a new state. Blacksmiths and other craftsmen provided the tools needed for trade, building, and other important tasks, as well as weapons for military conflicts. Their impressive natural resources provided the money necessary to centralize their power and expand their influence over their neighbors.

Maghan Kon Fatta

In their tales of pre-imperial Mali, griots tell of Maghan Kon Fatta, the Malian king also known as Maghan the Handsome, who received a mysterious hunter at his court one day. The hunter uttered a prophecy that, if the king married an ugly woman, she would bear him a son who would become a mighty ruler. Maghan Kon Fatta already had a first wife, Sassouma Berete. However, he took the prophecy seriously. When two Traoré hunters from the Do kingdom presented him an ugly, hunchbacked woman named Sogolon, Maghan remembered the prophecy and married her. She soon gave birth to a son, Sundiata, who was unable to walk throughout most of his childhood. Despite this deformity, Maghan insisted that Sundiata, and not his healthy son from the first marriage, assume the throne after his death. According to Sundiata's epic, the king's actions would set the stage for his small kingdom to grow into a mighty empire under the eventual leadership of his son, Sundiata.

CHAPTER TWO

Sundiata: Founder of the Empire

The *Sundiata Keita* ("Epic of Sundiata") is an epic poem that tells the story of Sundiata, a legendary hero who is credited with the founding of the Empire of Mali. The epic derives from oral tradition and has been told and passed down by griots for hundreds of years, since the fourteenth century. The tale originated with the Malinke people, who are also known as the Mandinka, one of the largest ethnic groups in West Africa.

The story of Sundiata is the most famous of all Malian griot epics. It begins with Sundiata's father, the handsome king Maghan Kon Fatta, whose family had ruled for three centuries. Sundiata's mother was Sogolon Kedjou, an ugly hunchback who, before she married, could transform herself into a buffalo. When he was born, Sundiata was named Sogolon-Djata, meaning "son of the lion and the buffalo." He was born lame and sick, and, by the age of seven, Sogolon-Djata was still unable to walk.

The Empire of Ghana, of which Mali was a part, was then ruled by Sumanguru, king of the Susu. He had seized control during the chaos caused when minor kings in the empire competed for power. In the early 1200s, Sumanguru attacked Kangaba in order to capture its slaves. He spared the young Sundiata's life because the child could not walk. Before departing, however, Sumanguru insulted the Mandinka, calling them weak and spineless, just like the king's son.

Sundiata Stands Up

Sogolon-Djata often had to watch his mother suffer humiliation because of his deformed leg and her hunchback. The day came when he could endure no more. He asked his loyal griot, Balla Fasseke, to enlist the royal blacksmiths to make a heavy iron rod. The rod was so heavy that six apprentices were needed to carry it to Sogolon-Djata. He crawled on all-fours to the iron rod, then grasped it, leaned on it, and lifted himself up into a standing position.

Soglon-Djata's effort and exertion had been so great that he bent the iron bar into a bow shape while pulling himself up. In one mighty movement, Soglon-Djata stood tall and became a powerful hunter, as symbolized by the bow. His first steps were said to be those of a giant. Through his courage and determination, Sogolon-Djata grew to be a brave hunter and warrior. His name was shortened to Sundiata, which means "the hungering lion."

Sundiata Victorious

Sundiata became king of Mali in 1230. As king, Sundiata decided to free Mali from the tyranny of Sumanguru. A griot praise-song attributes the following inspiring words to Sundiata, uttered to his followers on the eve of battle: "I salute you all, sons of Mali! As long as I breathe, Mali will never be in slavery—rather death than slavery. We will be free

A sculpture of a Malian warrior is armed with a spear.

because our ancestors were free. I am going to avenge the indignity that Mali has suffered."

Sundiata's final victory over Sumanguru took place on the plain at the Battle of Kirina in 1235. According to griot legend, this was a resounding victory for Sundiata, and his army rapidly conquered a vast area. Mali's new territory was approximately three times the size of the former Empire of Ghana.

Sundiata established an efficient system of government by appointing loyal governors to rule distant provinces. He absorbed several lesser kings into his empire, allowing them to continue ruling their own areas while they acknowledged his authority. These kings paid Sundiata an annual tribute, a tax on produce and other valuable goods. After Sundiata brought peace to this region, known as the Western Sudan, its people put down their arms and returned to farming and trade.

The Niger River's delta enabled farming and had protected the Ghanaians from drought, although severe drought might have been one key factor in their downfall. The Niger River also served as a quick transportation route, allowing trade throughout the region and contributing to the wealth of both the Ghanaian and Malian empires.

Mali and Islam

For many centuries, trade across the Sahara Desert had been conducted mainly by Berber peoples, including the Tuareg. Arab Muslim armies that had invaded the North African coast conquered the Berbers in the seventh century. Over the next five hundred years, Islamic civilization led the world in learning, art, science, government, and trade.

The Berbers, however, regained control from the Arabs. Led by the Fatimids, a Muslim dynasty from Yemen, and supported by soldiers from the Western Sudan, the Berbers conquered Egypt in 969 and built their capital in Cairo, Egypt. For a time, Fatimid Berbers played a leading role in the Muslim world, which spread from North Africa to Syria and into parts of Arabia.

By the time of Sundiata's victory over Sumanguru in 1235, the Berber empire had splintered. The Berbers were unable to unify and fully control North Africa. The center of Berber power was in Tunis, located in present-day Tunisia. A web of trade routes linked Tunis with the great cities of the Sahel, including Niani, Timbuktu, Jenne, and Gao, which were controlled by the Empire of Mali.

Shown here are ancient Arab manuscripts rediscovered and secured for restoration in Bouj Beha, Mali, including a Koran dating from 1423 CE.

Malian cities were populated by a mixture of peoples, including Muslims and Berber traders. Historians believe that, unlike Sumanguru, Sundiata adopted Islam, perhaps partly to restore the confidence of Muslim Berber merchants. They had halted trade when the Empire of Ghana was plunged into war. Like Sundiata, many merchants in the Empire of Mali also converted to Islam. This facilitated trade relations with Berbers to the north. Islamic scholarship also took root in the Empire of Mali, particularly in Timbuktu. In the countryside, however, many still observed traditional religions.

NIANI: CAPITAL OF THE EMPIRE

Sundiata established a new capital on the Niger River at Niani, his birthplace, although Kangaba remained the spiritual center of the Mali Empire. Formerly, Niani had been an administrative center of the Empire of Ghana. The praise-songs of the griots portray Niani as a city of great wealth and power. Arabic writers have described Niani's houses, constructed of clay with roofs of wood and reed, and the king's palace, which was surrounded by a wall. Archaeologists know the general location of Niani but have yet to confirm the exact location. A 1965 joint expedition by a Polish and Guinean team revealed ruins in the area that suggested that human settlements had existed at Niani since at least the sixth century CE.

Sundiata: King of Kings

Under Sundiata, the Empire of Mali played a key role in world affairs, then dominated by Muslims. In fact, much of the world's economy depended on gold from the Empire of Mali. During Sundiata's peaceful and prosperous reign, the Mali Kingdom grew into a powerful empire.

Following his defeat of Sumanguru and the consequent fall of the Ghanaian Empire, Sundiata became the first emperor of Mali. In doing so, he became the first in the long line of Malian kings to use the royal title "Mansa," which means "king of kings" in the Mandinka language. He quickly set about expanding his empire. With the help of his chief general, Tiramakhan, Sundiata seized territory in present-day Senegal, Gambia, and Guinea Bissau.

Far from being an oppressive dictator, Sundiata seems to have overseen a comparatively enlightened monarchy. He routinely consulted with a federation of tribal chiefs and voluntarily had his power checked by the Great Gbara Assembly—a deliberative body created by Sundiata in the Mandika constitution (the "Kouroukan Fouga"). Sundiata's commitment to constitutionally based and representative good government, along with his development of agriculture (he is credited with introducing weaving and cotton to Mali), is what helped build his empire and ensure his legacy. Both are still revered today, in West Africa and worldwide.

CHAPTER THREE

A Fertile and Industrious Empire

Several factors were key to the success of the Mali Empire. Its agricultural abundance, geography, and resources all played vital roles. Unlike the older Empire of Ghana, which relied primarily on the donkey, horse, and camel for transporting food and goods over land, Malians had the additional benefit of access to the Niger River.

The Niger's river basin provided fertile lands and a more convenient way of moving people and products. This allowed the transport of much greater loads much faster than via land. The empire's other great sources of wealth came from trade and its substantial natural resources, especially its gold. These factors combined to strengthen the empire and ensure greater stability than the Ghanaians had enjoyed.

Agriculture and Weaving

Farming has always been the economic foundation of the Mandé world. West Africans were already cultivating crops by the end of the second millennium BCE, making them among the world's earliest farmers. Some scholars even theorize that the larger Mandé group of peoples were the first in West Africa to develop highly organized forms of agriculture much earlier, between about 4000 BCE and 3000 BCE.

A woman carries containers through onion fields in the Dogon region of Mali, not far from the sandstone Bandiagara Escarpment, a place designated as a UNESCO World Heritage Site.

Cotton, sesame, sorghum, and millet were just some of the crops grown in this region. The people of the empire also grew beans, rice, papaya, gourds, and peanuts. Livestock raised in the empire included sheep, poultry, goats, and cattle. Sundiata's son, Mansa Wali, is said to have encouraged farming as his father had. By the time of Wali's death in 1270, the Empire of Mali had developed extensive and rich farming areas and was producing a surplus of food for export. In some cases, slaves were used as labor to clear the forested lands needed for agriculture.

Particularly important to the Malians was cotton, which was spun and used to weave cloth. In Mandé culture and mythology, weaving is considered a divine gift, first taught to humans by spiders. Archaeological evidence suggests that Mandé-speaking peoples have produced woven cotton cloth for at least one thousand years. Today, Mandé men continue the ancient craft, passing on to their sons the skill of weaving long, narrow strips of cloth on horizontal looms. The woven strips can be stitched together to form a large cloth. In the past, these strips were widely used as a form of currency, while textiles were important trade items.

Skilled Craftwork

In the Sundiata epic, an iron bar finally allows Sundiata to stand on his own two feet. Similarly, the strength of African kingdoms from 500 CE onward depended on iron. Iron tools and weapons produced by skilled blacksmiths enabled farmers, hunters, and warriors to feed and protect their people. The weapons used by the empire's army included iron-tipped spears, daggers, swords, and bows and arrows. Blacksmiths also provided wooden objects for defense, such as battle clubs.

Then and now, blacksmiths held a special place in Mandé society. Their ability to transform rocks containing iron ore into tools by using fire, air, and water was seen as evidence of great spiritual power. Blacksmiths were so respected for their apparently supernatural abilities that they were also called upon to play other roles in their communities. They served as doctors, spiritual guides, political advisers, and interpreters. In addition, as the empire expanded, blacksmiths often established lodges, or secret societies, within host communities. These lodges provided spiritual leadership and protection to the community's members and oversaw the repair and maintenance of bridges and roads.

Scholars of the period also recognized just how important Mandé blacksmiths' skills were in conveying not only the spiritual power of their people, but also the technological and cultural superiority of the Mandé. Their skills were crucial for maintaining the empire's military and agricultural advantages over its rivals.

The efforts of leatherworkers also contributed to the empire's success. The saddles, bridles, sword sheaths, protective wear, and other garments they crafted, alongside the weaponry

This is a "charm gown," or hunter's shirt, of the Bambara people.

of the blacksmiths, were a major factor in the superior cavalry of the Malian Empire, and its military in general. These skilled craftsmen of the Mandé helped the empire effectively control its vast territories.

Like griots and weavers, blacksmiths passed their skills and mystical knowledge from one generation to the next, often to their sons and nephews. Mandé blacksmiths' wives often were (and still are) skilled potters. They form clay from the earth into large vessels and fire them in open-air kilns. Such pots are used for carrying water, cooking, and storing food.

HUNTER'S SHIRTS

Mandé blacksmiths made hunter's shirts, which are still produced and worn today. Several charms are attached to each shirt for protection and to promote success in hunting and battle. The charms include mirrors, claws, horns filled with magical medicines, and protective amulets—small leather pouches containing passages from the Koran, the holy text of the Muslims. The more charms on a shirt, the greater the hunter's physical and supernatural powers and the more likely he was to be a great leader. The first kings of Mali are described as hunter-warrior kings, and the Sundiata epic relates that both Sundiata and his griot, Balla Fasseke, wore hunter's shirts. In modern Mali, hunter's shirts also serve as a kind of formal wear to distinguish hunters within the community during parades, festivals, rituals, and other special gatherings.

A Crossroads of Global Trade

Like the Empire of Ghana before it, the Empire of Mali owed much of its success to its strategic location in the Sahel. It was situated between the gold mines in the southern forests and the salt mines in the Sahara Desert. In Arabic, *sahel* means "shore." If the Sahara can be considered a vast sea of sand, the towns on the southern edge of the desert were like coastal ports, to which camels—the ships of the desert—brought goods.

Mali's main sources of mineral wealth were the Wangara gold mines and the salt mines of Taghaza. From Sundiata's reign until the 1500s, gold from the Malian Empire was the main source for the manufacture of coins in the Muslim world. Europe also received its gold mainly from Muslim suppliers. Hence, much of the world's currency depended on the Empire of Mali. It is estimated that as much as two-thirds of the world's gold supplies originated in the empire's mines.

Donkey and camel caravans brought many other goods to the cities of the empire. Among the items traded were slaves, horses, livestock, textiles, books, tools, wood, leather goods, ivory, perfumes, rare birds, beads, jewelry, honey, milk, rice, millet, fish, kola nuts, shea nuts, silver, tin, lead, and other metals.

Trade introduced Mali's riches to Europe, Arabia, and Asia. In return, rare and precious items from these regions were brought to Mali. Scholars, poets, ambassadors, and musicians traveled together with merchants in the camel caravans. As trade flourished, camel stops along the vast network of these

A man trails behind a camel caravan transporting goods across the harsh Malian Sahara. Trade via camel still occurs through the desert, even though it has largely been replaced elsewhere by mechanical means.

routes grew into towns.

The empire also used crops and other goods and commodities as forms of currency, including cotton cloth, salt, gold, and even gold dust. The smaller kingdoms that swore allegiance to Mali paid annual tributes to the emperor in the form of crafted items such as lances and arrows, as well as agricultural ones like rice and millet. Like the Ghanaians before them, the Malians also prospered from the taxes they imposed on the trade they controlled and allowed in their territory.

CHAPTER FOUR

The Reign of Mansa Musa

As glorious as the reign of its first emperor had been, Mali's influence would only continue to grow. Its greatest and most influential era was still to come. Nevertheless, the empire would endure a crisis of succession before it reached its greatest heights. Sundiata died an accidental death in 1255. His son, Mansa Wali, rose to the throne and ruled until he himself passed away in 1270.

After Mansa Wali's death, the Empire of Mali was plunged into uncertainty as several possible leaders struggled for power. In 1307, a grandson of one of Sundiata's sisters assumed the throne. His name was Musa, which means "Moses" in Arabic, a name that foreshadowed his future role as an influential leader.

During the reign of Mansa Musa, who became one of Africa's most famous kings, the size of the Mali Empire doubled and its volume of trade tripled. New gold mines were discovered farther to the east. Sagaman-dir, the commander of Mansa Musa's army, captured Gao, the capital of the neighboring city-state of Songhay. This military victory gave Mali control of the copper mines of Tadmekka. Mansa Musa is reported to have said that copper was the main source of his wealth.

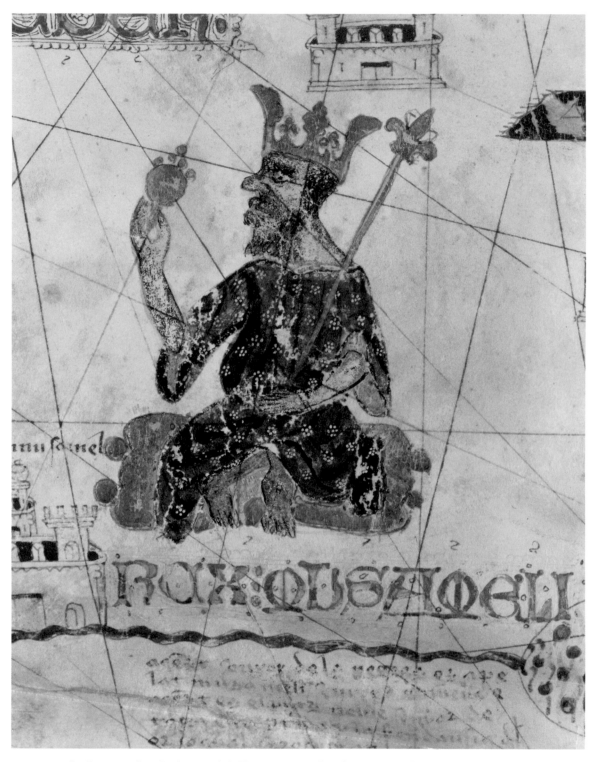

Toward the end of the Middle Ages, the image of Mansa Musa was known in both the Islamic and non-Islamic worlds. His wealth and fame inspired his depiction on European atlases and maps, such as this one.

An Islamic State

In 1312, motivated in part by a desire to strengthen trade with the Arab world, Mansa Musa made Islam the official religion of the Mali Empire. He welcomed Arabs to his kingdom. In Mali, the ulama, meaning "the learned," who were the officials and teachers of Islam, became politically powerful in the cities. While embracing Islam, Mansa Musa continued to respect the traditional African religions that most of his subjects in the countryside observed. He did not forcibly convert others to Islam.

A Legendary Pilgrimage

In 1324, Mansa Musa set off across the desert with an enormous entourage. He was following his Muslim obligation to undertake the hajj. It was to be one of the most famous journeys ever undertaken in world history.

Estimates of the number of people who accompanied him vary from eight thousand to sixty thousand. Among these were many of the empire's princes, chiefs, and military leaders. This was partly to prevent them from sowing unrest in his absence. He also took his wife, together with her five hundred attendants. They crossed the desert, taking with them an enormous herd of animals to provide transport and food. Five hundred slaves each carried a 6-pound (2.7-kilogram) staff of gold. Hundreds of camels carried food, clothing, supplies, and about 30,000 pounds (14,000 kg) of gold.

Mansa Musa's caravan amazed everyone who saw it. Egyptian author al-Umari described it as "a lavish display of power and wealth that was unprecedented in its size and pageantry." In keeping with a precept of Islam that the rich must share their wealth with the poor, Mansa Musa gave away a great deal of gold on his journey. In fact, he gave away so much in Cairo that the price of gold dropped in the city and surrounding region. It is said that prices in Cairo were so disrupted that it took more than twelve years for Egypt's economy to recover from Mansa Musa's visit.

Mansa Musa's pilgrimage cemented relationships with Egypt and the Muslim world to the east. It also encouraged immigration and brought visitors to Mali's cities. While in

A man rides a donkey past the Sankore mosque in the city of Timbuktu, Mali. This structure dates from the fifteenth or sixteenth century CE. Imperial-era architectural treasures such as this remain throughout the country.

Mecca, Mansa Musa met Abu Ishaq es-Saheli, an Arab architect and poet from southern Spain. He returned to Mali with Mansa Musa and designed several royal palaces for him, as well as the famous Sankore mosque in Timbuktu.

Timbuktu was an important center of trade and learning during this period. The city had a large international population of merchants, artisans, and scholars, most of whom were Muslims. Sankore University, boasting famous libraries of Arabic texts, was located there. It was in the universities of the Muslim world such as Timbuktu that many classical texts of ancient Greece and Rome were also preserved. Many copies of these texts had been forgotten, lost, or destroyed in Europe following the fall of the Roman Empire in the early fifth century CE. This lost knowledge wasn't

THE HEIGHT OF THE EMPIRE

Toward the end of Mansa Musa's reign, the empire had reached its greatest strength and influence. By about 1350, the empire held sway over more than four hundred cities, towns, and villages, with some historians estimating a total population of about twenty million people. Its army numbered about one hundred thousand men, with a cavalry of ten thousand. At the height of its power, the Empire of Mali stretched almost 2,000 miles (3,200 kilometers), from the Atlantic Ocean in the west to beyond Gao and the bend of the Niger River in the east, and from the southern edge of the Sahara to the southern forest belt.

reintroduced to Europe until the Renaissance, thanks in large measure to the archival efforts of Muslim scholars.

A Fair and Just Ruler

Historian al-Umari reported in 1325 that Mansa Musa held court on a wide balcony. He sat on a great wooden throne placed between elephant tusks and wore trousers of sewn cloth strips in an exclusive pattern. Mansa Musa was surrounded by his weapons, all made of gold, and a dozen Turkish slaves, one of whom shaded him with a silk umbrella.

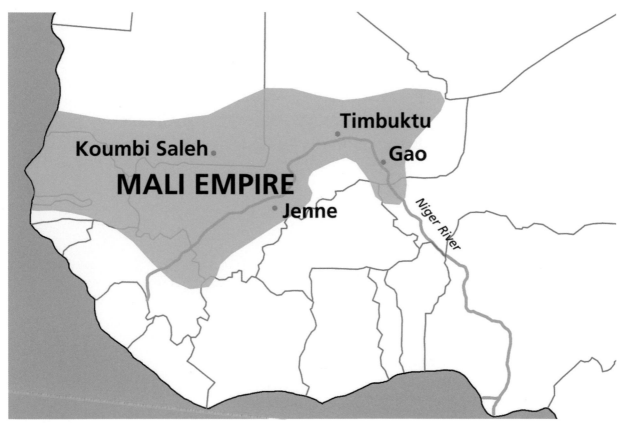

This map depicts the extent of the Mali Empire around 1350 CE. It features the major urban and cultural centers of the time, including Timbuktu, Gao, Jenne, and Koumbi Saleh, believed to have been a capital of the Ghanaian Empire.

Ibn Battuta visited the court of Mali a few decades later. He found that the women of Mali were treated with more respect than those of other nations and enjoyed greater freedoms than other Muslim women. Ibn Battuta also commented on the safety that citizens, travelers, and visitors alike enjoyed within the empire and the commitment to fairness and justice demonstrated by Mansa Musa and his laws.

According to some eyewitness accounts written during the height of the Malian Empire, journeying from one end of the realm to the other required eight months of travel. Even though some of its territory included desert regions, most of the empire was said to have been inhabited, with over four hundred cities, towns, and villages spread throughout the realm. At its zenith in the mid-fourteenth century, the Empire of Mali extended throughout present-day Senegal, southern Mauritania, Mali, northern Burkina Faso, western Niger, the Gambia, Guinea-Bissau, Guinea, the Ivory Coast, and northern Ghana. At this time, only the Mongol Empire was larger.

CHAPTER FIVE

The Fall of a Vulnerable Empire

Even as the Empire of Mali enjoyed great power because of its resources and trade, it was that very success that helped plant the seeds of its demise. The smaller kingdoms that swore allegiance to Mali wanted a greater share of the wealth that commerce in salt and gold had yielded. Among the first challenges to imperial power was a rebellion by the Wolof people, who lived in the part of the empire now known as Senegal.

After Mansa Musa's death, his son, Maghan, became king. During his four-year reign, another serious setback occurred when Tuareg forces captured Timbuktu in 1430. For an enemy to capture the richest city of the empire signaled a loss of prestige. This humiliating defeat further weakened the empire's already shaky standing and inspired others who wished to rebel against it. The capture of Timbuktu exposed the Empire of Mali's vulnerability to attack. In the next century, the empire was besieged from all sides.

By the mid-1400s, Mali had lost its northern provinces to the Tuareg Berbers, losing control over the Saharan trade. In the west, the Tucolor and Wolof city-states revolted against Mali, with the latter declaring its own empire, the Empire of Jolof, in 1380. Mali's southern trade routes and market towns were attacked by Mossi cavalry from 1430 to 1483. In the

La caravane de Touareg au Vélodrome d'hiver

This illustrated newspaper supplement from 1753 shows a group of Tuareg tribesmen dressed in traditional clothing and resting at their desert oasis encampment during a wintertime desert crossing.

eastern region of Gao, however, the Songhay Empire, independent since the late 1300s, was consolidating its power. Soon it would emerge as the next great West African empire.

The Growing Influence of Europe

As the Empire of Mali peaked and then began to disintegrate and crumble, Arab world power was on the decline, while European power and influence was resurgent. Europe's awareness of and interest in Africa had grown steadily.

From the eighth century onward, Berbers and Arabs had conquered and ruled much of the Iberian Peninsula, which included Spain and Portugal. Along with other mostly Muslim North and West Africans, these groups were collectively known to the Europeans as the Moors. They intermarried with Spaniards and the Portuguese. The Moors preserved and reintroduced much of the knowledge that had been lost to Europe during the so-called Dark Ages that followed the barbarian invasions. Not all of this cross-cultural influence was positive, however. From the 1200s onward, more and more Africans were sold into slavery in European cities such as Genoa, Naples, and Barcelona.

In the fourteenth century, Europeans were eager to establish direct contact with the wealthy Empire of Mali, rather than buy their gold and other African goods from Muslim traders. The first European map of West Africa, drawn in 1375 for Charles V of France by a Majorcan mapmaker, shows how large Mansa Musa loomed in the European imagination. Wearing a gold crown and holding a golden staff, Mansa Musa's figure dominates the map. In his out-stretched hand he displays a gold nugget; a trader approaches on a camel. It is possible that Mansa Musa inspired European artists in the fourteenth century to portray one of the Three Wise Men in the New Testament as an African king.

By the fifteenth century, some Europeans had established direct ties with the Empire of Mali. One was Anselme d'Isaguier, a nobleman trader and politician from Toulouse, France. He married Salam Casais, the daughter of a Songhay chief and a member of a wealthy, influential family in Gao, then controlled by Mali. Salam Casais traveled back to

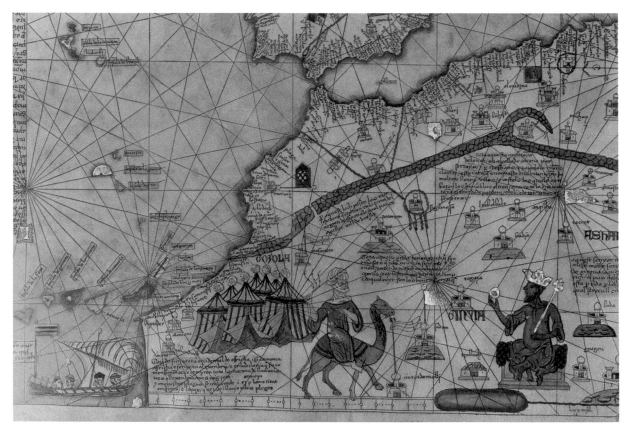

A detail of the Catalan Atlas of 1375, named after Spain's Catalan region, depicts much of North Africa during the last days of the Empire of Mali and its regional dominance.

France with him, accompanied by six Malian attendants. They crossed the Sahara and then sailed the Mediterranean, finally arriving in France in 1413. One of Salam Casais's companions was Aben Ali, a medical doctor. He became so renowned in France that in 1419 he treated Prince Charles, heir to the French throne.

Florence, Italy, was the leading commercial and cultural center of southern Europe in the mid-1400s. In 1469, a Florentine bank sent Benedetto Dei, an agent of the Portinari company, to Timbuktu to negotiate a trade agreement with the mansa. Europe had finally established direct commercial relations with the Empire of Mali.

European Colonization of Africa

The Portuguese were the first Europeans to sail around the bulge of West Africa, in 1471. The voyage was made possible when the Portuguese began using the lateen, a type of triangular sail then identified mainly with Arab seafaring.

The Portuguese, rapidly followed by other European powers, established trading posts along the African coast, where they could now obtain gold, slaves, and African products. There was no longer a need to trade with Muslim merchants or risk the perils of the Sahara Desert. Though some trade still flowed across the Sahara (and continues today), the Atlantic trade grew rapidly and weakened the influence of the great cities of the Sahel. African peoples along the Atlantic coast grew wealthy from direct trade with Europeans.

Le drapeau français arboré à Tombouctou

This engraving, published in *Le Petit Journal* in 1894, shows victorious French troops at the raising of France's tricolor flag in Timbuktu. A few years later, France took control of much of West Africa.

European colonization of the Americas also affected Africa. After Europeans found new sources of gold in the New World, African gold became secondary as a trade good to the value of the African slave trade. Europeans now began to import large numbers of slaves to work the plantations they established in the new colonies of the Americas.

FRENCH COLONIAL MALI

It was toward the end of the nineteenth century, during the era of European colonialism, when France conquered a huge part of West Africa. Part of this conquered territory was called French Sudan, which encompassed much of Mali and its neighboring states. Mali's colonial period, from 1892 to 1960, was marked by several revolts and French control over its agricultural and natural resources.

One result of the colonial era is that French is spoken in much of West Africa. Even today, it remains the primary official language of Mali and the most widely spoken nationwide. The French built railroads and other infrastructure, which they used mainly to transport the cotton, peanuts, and other goods they forced many Malians to produce. Aside from this industrial activity, much of the country remained undeveloped. Despite the oppressive nature of French colonialism, the Malians kept alive their religion, skilled trades, and traditions into the modern era.

An Empire Falls, but the Legacy Endures

Like the earlier Empire of Ghana, the Empire of Mali gradually disintegrated because of internal conflict and foreign aggression. The Empire of Songhay later rose in its place. Greatly diminished, Mali maintained control of the gold fields of Bambuk until the end of the 1500s, when the Empire of Songhay also began to collapse.

Much changed, naturally, between the decline of the Empire of Mali and the present day. After Mali's imperial power faded, the main power in West Africa belonged to the Songhay Empire, which established its capital at Gao. By the late 1460s, the Songhay ruler, Sunni Ali, had conquered much of Mali's remaining territory, including Timbuktu and other cities. After the Songhays declined, power over Mali's former empire belonged to a succession of different kingdoms.

Mansa Mahmud IV was the last emperor of Manden. He fought valiantly against the far better-equipped forces of the Moroccan Pashalik of Timbuktu in 1599. The Moroccans went into battle with firearms, a new technology that would radically alter the balance of power in Africa, contributing to the fall of both the Malian and the Songhay empires. Following Mahmud's retreat and eventual death, his three sons vied for power and the empire was divided into three smaller territories with no imperial unity or central governance. The once mighty and awe-inspiring Empire of Mali was no more.

CHAPTER SIX

Mali Today

Though the Empire of Mali had declined, the fame of its wealth, power, and cultural achievements never faded from memory. Tales of Mansa Musa's fabulous hajj have been told in Africa and the Muslim world for generations.

Today, the Western Sudan is divided into many countries, most of which were ruled by France until their independence in 1960. The modern nation of Mali, which includes the cities of Timbuktu, Gao, and Jenne, was named in honor of the Empire of Mali.

The modern nation of Mali owes much to its rich history and cultural heritage. Traditions with origins extending as far back as Mali's preimperial history still remain strong. Meanwhile, changes experienced within the last century have contributed to a diverse and dynamic modern nation.

Mali gained independence from France in 1960. A military dictatorship ran the country from 1969 until democratic elections were held in 1992. In the two decades since, despite being one of the poorer states in Africa, Mali gained a reputation as a stable and democratic nation known for religious and ethnic tolerance.

Residents of Mali's capital of Bamako negotiate traffic during the tense times of the uprising of Tuareg separatists in the north.

North and South

When modern Mali took shape, it shared some of the same territories as its ancient empire. Nowadays, it is a landlocked country, with much of the population centered around the Niger River delta. The nation's larger northern region adjoins and is part of the vast Sahara Desert, comprising a territory called Azawad, which accounts for about 60 percent of the country's land. Because of its arid climate, it is much less densely populated than southern Mali.

The vast majority of Malians—around 90 percent—reside in the south, with large concentrations around the capital, Bamako, and other large cities. Urban life in Mali resembles that of the rest of developed, industrialized Africa and other western cities. In rural Mali, many people still maintain a traditional, village-oriented way of life.

The main groups living in the northern Azawad region are the Tuareg and Moor (or Maur) peoples, who have traditionally been a nomadic people, a way of life common in the Sahara. Tuaregs have historically been suspicious of central government control and have attempted to gain their independence at various times. Tuaregs are largely descended from Berber peoples, while the Moors have a mixed Arab/Berber heritage.

Language

Cultural and ethnic differences exist within Mali today, both between the north and south and among other groups concentrated in its southern regions. Various ethnicities of the Mandé people still make up at least half of the modern nation's population, including the Bambara, Malinke, and Soninke subgroups. Other significant minorities include the Fulbe (or Fulani), Voltaic, Songhai, and Tuareg and Moor peoples, according to the latest population and demographic data reported in the CIA's *World Factbook.*

French is the official language of Mali and is spoken universally. About 80 percent of Malians speak Bambara, while a total of thirteen indigenous languages are considered national languages in Mali. In addition many more languages are also spoken in Mali.

With such a multicultural and multiethnic history, it is unsurprising that Malians have a tolerant, inclusive society. Most Malians are Sunni Muslims who adhere to Sufism, a type of Islamic practice that stresses mysticism, dance, specific rituals, and open-mindedness. There is no official state religion, and the practice of Islam in different villages and among ethnic subgroups varies. A small segment of the population (about 5 percent) are Christian.

The Conflict in Mali

In January 2012, Tuareg separatists, who had long sought their independence from the southern-based central government in Bamako, started a revolt in the Azawad region. The National Movement for the Liberation of Azawad (MNLA) hoped to make northern Mali a separate Tuareg homeland. In March 2012, President Toumani Touré was thrown out of power in a coup d'état orchestrated by those angry at him for not responding strongly to the crisis.

The cities of Timbuktu, Kidal, and Gao and neighboring regions were captured by MNLA forces, who had allied themselves with Ansar Dine, an Islamist group that favored strict Sharia law. Having achieved their shared goal of overthrowing President Touré, these rebel forces would later turn against each other because Ansar Dine and the MNLA differed on many issues.

Eventually, in January 2013, French military forces assisted the Malian military and together recaptured much of the north.

THE GREAT MOSQUE OF JENNE

Among the most important, culturally significant, and recognizable sites in Mali is the Great Mosque of Jenne, located in the town of Jenne near the Bani River. As an Islamic center, the town and mosque were most active and influential in the fifteenth and sixteenth centuries. Archaeologists estimate that the structure, the world's largest adobe (mud brick) building, may have been erected as early as the beginning of the thirteenth century. Surrounding areas have been inhabited since the third century BCE. This includes Jenne-Jenno, the town's original site, which, along with the mosque and nearby structures, has been designated a World Heritage Site by the United Nations Educational, Scientific, and Cultural Organization (UNESCO). With its mix of buildings and artifacts from the nation's pre-Islamic and Islamic eras, the area truly exemplifies Mali's rich and diverse history.

With a French troop withdrawal beginning in April 2013, African Union soldiers, members of a peacekeeping force drawn from several African nations, were charged with helping the Malian troops maintain the uneasy calm. The conflict has subsided for now but has left hundreds dead and more than three hundred thousand displaced.

The cultural cost has also been high. The Islamic fundamentalists of Ansar Dine are blamed for destroying or attempting to destroy ancient artifacts and religious sites of Sufis and other

Muslims and non-Muslims who don't share their beliefs. They also banned music and musicians in conquered areas.

Preserving Islamic Treasures

The recent conflict and the controversy surrounding it has shed light on the deep pride that Malians feel for their ancient cultural heritage, especially their age-old collections of precious Islamic artifacts and documents. *Time* magazine reported in January 2013 how scholars, preservationists, and even private citizens had worked together to hide thousands of rare

Malians pass by the famous Great Mosque of Jenne, one of the most distinctive and revered ancient sites of Muslim learning and worship in the world. UNESCO designated the mosque and surrounding sites as a World Heritage Site in 1988.

documents from invading troops, including members of Al Qaeda in the Islamic Maghreb (AQIM), who had allied with the MNLA and Ansar Dine. When these troops took Timbuktu and were later forced to retreat, they burned many important sites as they fled, including the Ahmed Baba Institute, an important center of education and Islamic research. Luckily, many irreplaceable items had been hidden away beforehand.

Mali's Economy

Mali's modern economy depends on many of the same activities that provided wealth during its imperial days: agriculture and mining. According to the World Bank and International Monetary Fund (IMF), about 80 percent of the population earns a living through farming or fishing, including food processing.

In recent years, the nation has attempted to expand its production of cotton, which is its main export. Other major export items include tobacco, tea, oils, and textiles. Gold is still a major economic resource, with iron ore extract a growing industry, as is the mining of salt, diamonds, tin, uranium, and other materials.

The nomadic population of the Malian north—about 10 percent of the nation's total population—survives mostly through herding animals. A small percentage of Mali's population earns a living from tourism, including the sale of traditional handicrafts.

Music

Mali is famous throughout West Africa and internationally as a nation where music is valued and masterfully created. It is promoted both officially—by the government to encourage tourism and preserve its ancient cultures—and by local communities nationwide. From the continuing tradition of griots to a widespread love of the style known as Afro-pop and other forms of artistic expression, music is integral to the everyday life of Mali's people.

Malian musicians have made their mark on the world stage. One of the most notable, both because of his fame and his lineage, is Salif Keita. The popular Afro-pop singer and songwriter belongs to the Keita family line and is a direct descendant of Sundiata himself. Another Malian superstar, Ali Farka Touré—of mixed Songhay and Fula heritage—was known internationally as one of the greatest guitarists of all time before he died in 2006. He is famous for combining Malian music with American blues.

Other important artists from Mali include Amadou and Mariam, a blind musical duo who mix Malian traditions with a wide variety of world music sounds, and Tinariwen, a band of Tuareg players who have enjoyed international acclaim.

Mali's Music Festivals

With Mali's rich history of griots and indigenous music, it is no surprise that it regularly hosts two of the largest and most vibrant musical gatherings on the African continent. The Festival au Desert (Festival in the Desert) has been staged in northern Mali since 2001, first in the remote village of Essakane and later outside of Timbuktu. Its main attractions have been the traditional and modern music, art, and dance of the Tuareg people, as well those of other Malian musicians and artists.

Popular Malian musician Salif Keita performs in Barcelona, Spain. Because he descends from imperial founder Sundiata, Keita's career choice actually goes against ancient Malian traditions, in which royalty could never be singers or griots.

The other major music festival is the Festival sur le Niger (Niger River Festival), which is held in and around Segou, an ancient capital of the Bambara people. This festival is a showcase for regional culture, music, art, and oral traditions. Visitors enjoy traditional dances, masks, puppetry, and some of the most popular musicians from Mali and Africa at large.

A Proud Heritage

The glorious past of Mali continues to inspire popular musicians, filmmakers, writers, and artists in West Africa. Griots still recount the achievements of the Empire of Mali, though some of them feel that this great history is now being overshadowed by the problems of modern life. However, as long as the griots and modern musicians continue to sing about the Empire of Mali, each new generation will learn about one of the greatest civilizations the world has ever seen.

1076 CE   Almoravid Berbers defeat Empire of Ghana.

early 1200s   Sumanguru rules the fragmented Empire of Ghana and attacks Kangaba but spares Sundiata's life.

1230   Sundiata becomes king of Mali.

1235   Sundiata conquers Sumanguru's army.

1235–1255 Sundiata builds Empire of Mali; gold from Mali becomes source of gold for Muslim and European currency.

1255–1270   Reign of Mansa Wali, Sundiata's son; expansion of empire; growth in agricultural production.

1307–1332   Reign of Mansa Musa; empire doubles in size and trade triples; Muslim influence worldwide increases.

1312 Mansa Musa makes Islam the official religion of Mali.

1324 Mansa Musa begins his pilgrimage to Mecca.

1332 Mansa Maghan begins to rule; Timbuktu is later raided.

c. 1375–1400   Songhay asserts independence.

c. 1400–1480   Empire of Mali pressed by the Songhay and Tuareg; northern province breaks away; Jenne and Timbuktu assert independence; decline of Mali's power; empire raided by the Mossi.

1471 Portuguese arrive in West Africa.

1493–1495   An ambassador of the Portuguese king visits Mansa Mamudu.

c. 1590–1600   Collapse of the Empire of Mali.

1905 Most of Mali is under the colonial control of France and is part of French Sudan.

1959 French Sudan and Senegal unite to become the Mali Federation.

1960 The Mali Federation gains independence from France. Modibo Keïta becomes Mali's first president.

1968 The Keïta regime is overthrown in a bloodless coup led by Moussa Traoré. A military-led regime is established.

1991 Antigovernment, pro-democracy protests lead to a coup, and the Traoré regime is overthrown. Opposition parties are legalized, and a national congress of civil and political groups meets to draft a new constitution. Mali becomes known as one of the most socially and politically stable countries in Africa.

2012 A Tuareg rebellion begins in northern Mali, led by the National Movement for the Liberation of Azawad (MNLA). President Amadou Toumani Touré is overthrown by General Amadou Sanogo who believes Touré hasn't done enough to forcefully put down the Tuareg rebellion. The MNLA takes control of northern Mali and declares independence for the territory of Azawad, but its former allies—the Islamist groups Ansar Dine and Al Qaeda in the Islamic Maghreb—turn on the MNLA and try to impose Islamic law on northern Mali.

2013 French forces intervene at the request of the Sanogo government. French and Malian forces retake the north, including the northern provincial capitals and Timbuktu.

adobe A building material composed of sun-dried bricks of clay.

city-state A self-governing state consisting of a city and its surrounding territory.

entourage A group of persons who accompany someone.

griot A West African storyteller who passes on the history of a people through epic poems, songs, and tales.

hajj The Islamic pilgrimage to the holy city of Mecca.

humiliation The state of being lowered in status in others' eyes.

Islam One of the three major monotheistic world religions; Islam teaches that Allah is the one god.

kora A stringed instrument used by griots in Mali.

lateen A triangular cloth sail.

Maa Ngala According to ancient beliefs, the creator of the Mandé people.

Mandeblo A sacred shrine of the Mandé people.

Mandinka A West African people who built the Mali Empire.

mansa A king selected to rule the twelve Mandinka kingdoms.

Moors A collective name given by Europeans to describe the Muslims of North Africa; also, the name of a particular ethnic group of Mali.

negotiator One who settles a matter with others through discussion and compromise.

nomadic Characteristic of the lifestyles of nomads, people whose culture involves moving around regularly, rather than remaining in one place; roaming about from place to place aimlessly, frequently, or without a fixed pattern of movement.

plantation An estate or large farm on which workers cultivate crops.

preservationist Someone who works to save artifacts, buildings, and other examples of a nation's historical traditions and treasures.

renowned Famous or well known.

resurgent On the rise or increasing in influence or power.

Sahel In West Africa, the region lying between the Sahara Desert and the forest lands to the south.

sect One branch of a religion or religious belief system.

sharia A legal system based upon a very strict interpretation of Islamic law.

Sufism A branch of Islam that embraces mysticism and rituals.

surplus An extra amount of something.

textiles Woven natural or artificial materials used to make clothing or other useful goods.

tribute Payment in money or goods required of a subordinate people by their ruler.

FOR MORE INFORMATION

African Studies/Columbia University Libraries
Lehman Library
420 West 118th Street
New York, NY 10027
Web site: http://library.columbia.edu/indiv/global/
    africa.html
The African Studies Collections at Columbia University is
    one of the world's largest collections on African life,
    history, politics, and other subjects. Its Web site is a
    useful resource for further research on Mali and other
    African nations.

African Studies Center
University of California, Los Angeles (UCLA)
10244 Bunche Hall/405 Hilgard Avenue
Los Angeles, CA 90095
(310) 825-3686
Web site: http://www.international.ucla.edu/africa
The African Studies Center at UCLA declares its mission
    to be the critical and cultural study of the rapidly
    changing and complex face of Africa in the twenty-
    first century.

Canadian International Development Agency (CIDA)
200 Promenade du Portage
Gatineau, QC K1A 0G4
Canada
(819) 997-5456
Web site: http://www.acdi-cida.gc.ca/mali-e
The Canadian International Development Agency

provides development assistance to many nations around the world, including Mali, where it has had a presence since 1962.

Embassy of the Republic of Mali
2130 R Street NW
Washington, DC 20008
(202) 332-2249
Web site: http://www.maliembassy.us
The Embassy of the Republic of Mali is the nation's diplomatic
    mission to the United States, located in Washington, D.C.
    Its job is to promote Mali's cultural and political interests.

Embassy of the Republic of Mali (Canada)
50 Avenue Goulburn
Ottawa, ON K1N 8C8
Canada
(613) 232-1501
Web site: http://www.ambamalicanada.org
The Embassy of the Republic of Mali in Ottawa, Ontario, is the
    nation's Canadian diplomatic mission.

Malian Cultural Center
3130 Villa Avenue
Bronx, NY 10468
(347) 577-6330
Web site: http://umaca.org/about-us
The Malian Cultural Center, located in the Bronx, New York
    City, is a learning center and cultural advocacy organiza-
    tion for Malian immigrants to the United States.

Oxfam America
226 Causeway Street, 5th Floor
Boston, MA 02114-2206
(800) 77-OXFAM (776-9326)
Outside the US: (617) 482-1211
Web site: http://www.oxfam.org/en/development/mali
Oxfam is an international organization working to fight poverty. It has a significant presence in Mali and its West African neighbors.

Web Sites

Due to the changing nature of Internet links, Rosen Publishing has developed an online list of Web sites related to the subject of this book. This site is updated regularly. Please use this link to access the list:

http://www.rosenlinks.com/EAC/Mali

FOR FURTHER READING

Akyeampong, Emmanuel Kwaku, ed. *Themes in West Africa's History.* Athens, OH: Ohio University Press, 2006.

Armentrout, David. *Ghana, Mali, Songhay* (Timelines of Ancient Civilizations). Vero Beach, FL: Rourke Publishing, 2004.

Blauer, Ettagale, and Jason Laure. *Mali* (Cultures of the World). Tarrytown, NY: Marshall Cavendish, 2008.

Brook, Larry. *Daily Life in Ancient and Modern Timbuktu* (Cities Through Time). Minneapolis, MN: Runestone Press, 2000.

Conrad, David C. *Empires of Medieval West Africa* (Great Empires of the Past). New York, NY: Chelsea House, 2009.

de Villiers, Marq, and Sheila Hirtle. *Timbuktu: The Sahara's Fabled City of Gold.* New York, NY: Bloomsbury Publishing, 2009.

Dipiazza, Francesca Davis. *Mali in Pictures* (Visual Geography). Minneapolis, MN: Twenty-First Century Books, 2006.

Friedman, Mel. *Africa* (True Books). New York, NY: Children's Press, 2009.

Haywood, John. *West African Kingdoms* (Time Travel Guides). Mankato, MN: Heinemann-Raintree, 2008.

Koslow, Philip. *Mali: Crossroads of Africa* (Kingdoms of Africa). New York, NY: Chelsea House, 2000.

Marcovitz, Hal. *Islam in Africa* (Africa: Progress & Problems). Broomall, PA: Mason Crest Publishers, 2006.

McKissack, Patricia C., and Frederick McKissack. *The Royal Kingdoms of Ghana, Mali, and Songhay.* Clive, IA: Perfection Learning, 2010.

Mendonsa, Eugene L. *West Africa: An Introduction to Its History, Civilization, and Contemporary Situation.* Durham, NC: Carolina Academic Press, 2002.

Mitchell, Peter, ed. *West Africa* (Peoples and Cultures of Africa). New York, NY: Chelsea House, 2006.

Nardo, Dan. *The European Colonization of Africa* (World History). Greensboro, NC: Morgan Reynolds Publishing, 2010.

Pancella, Peggy. *Mansa Musa: Ruler of Ancient Mali* (Historical Biographies). Portsmouth, NH: Heinemann Library, 2003.

Sheehan, Sean. *Ancient African Kingdoms* (Exploring the Ancient World). New York, NY: Gareth Stevens Publishing, 2010.

Shuter, Jane. *Ancient West African Kingdoms* (History Opens Windows). Mankato, MN: Heinemann-Raintree, 2008.

Stone, Ruth M. *Music in West Africa: Experiencing Music, Expressing Culture.* New York, NY: Oxford University Press, 2004.

Woods, Michael. *Seven Wonders of Ancient Africa.* Minneapolis, MN: Twenty-First Century Books, 2008.

Worger, William H., et al. *Africa and the West: A Documentary History: Volume 1: From the Slave Trade to Conquest, 1441–1905.* New York, NY: Oxford University Press, 2010.

Worger, William H., et al. *Africa and the West: A Documentary History: Volume 2: From Colonialism to Independence, 1875 to the Present.* New York, NY: Oxford University Press, 2010.

Zamosky, Lisa. *Mansa Musa: Leader of Mali* (Primary Source Readers). Westminster, CA: Teacher Created Materials, 2008.

INDEX

About the Author

Philip Wolny is a writer from Queens, New York. His other Rosen titles covering culture and history include *Muslims Around the World* and *Colonialism: A Primary Source Analysis.*

Photo Credits